The grid method has been used by artists for centuries as a tool to creating correct proportions.
Renaissance artists, even the great Leonardo da Vinci, used the grid method!
The grid method dates back to the ancient Egyptians.
It is clearly a useful method for artists and aspiring artists alike.

The grid basically divides the original image into smaller blocks
so that you can more easily see what belongs where.
In this Sketchbook each square is 1 square cm.

The grid method can:
Help with capturing likeness from your image reference, with a focus on proportion.
Prevent you from drawing your object too large or small on the surface.
Make your planning and layout process a lot faster.

Why stick figures?

Stick figures:

- Are simple to draw and can be created on-the-spot.
- Create enthusiasm and trigger imagination and learner involvement.
- Can be used to provide multi-sensory learning experience.
- Provide symbolic representation of difficult concepts and help with contextualization.
- Add a visual context to new words learned thus enabling students to understand and remember new words and concepts better.

Stick figures are more than they seem. While they appear to be minimal representations of our children's outlook on life, they can, in fact, tell us a great deal about how our children feel, what they are thinking, how they see the world in which they live, how they see others, and how smart they might be.

Copyright © 2021

All rights reserved.

No part of this publication may be reproduced, distributed, or transmitted in any form or by any means including photocopying, recording, or other electronic or mechanical methods, without the prior written permission of the publisher.

ISBN: 9798747731431 (Paperback)

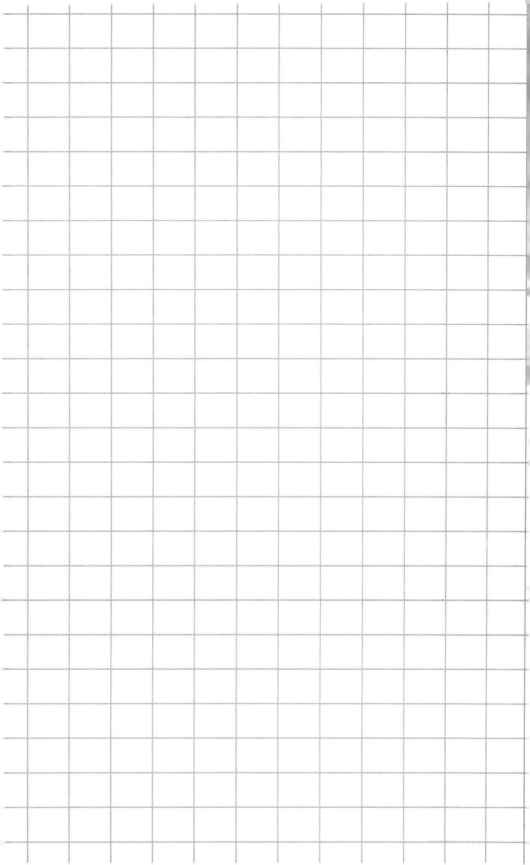

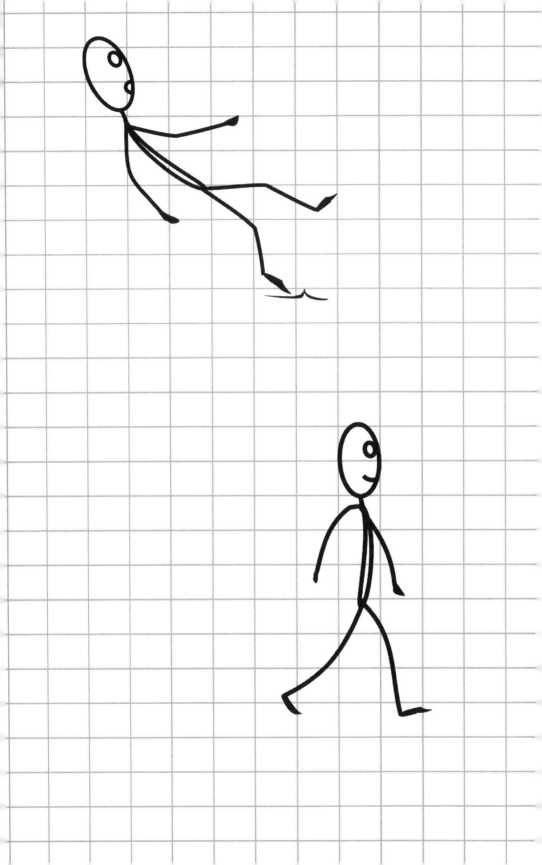

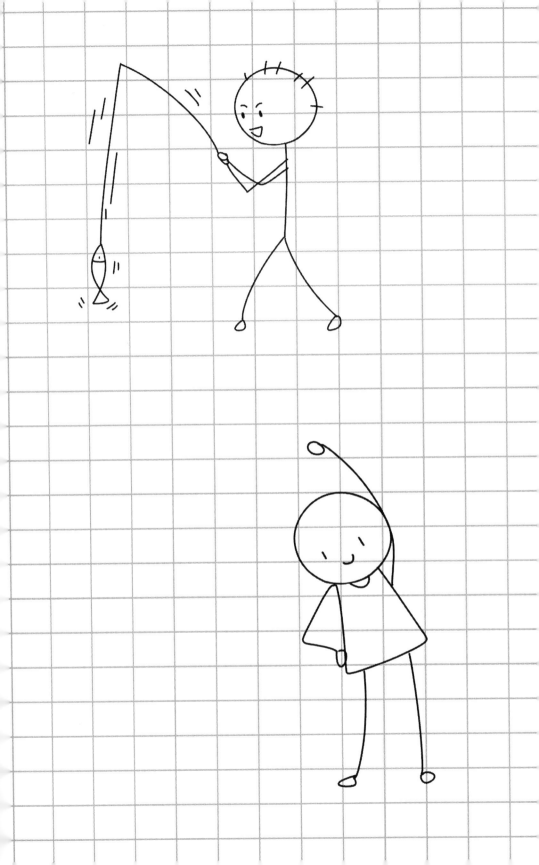

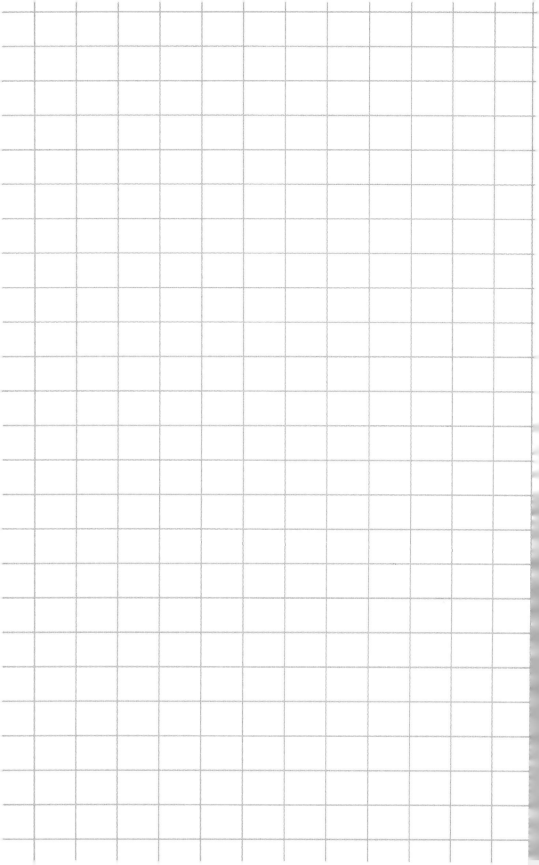

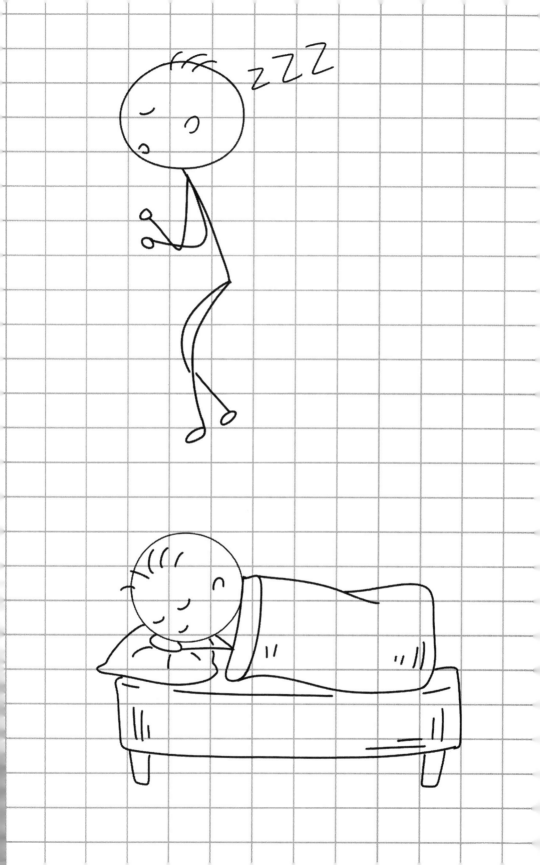

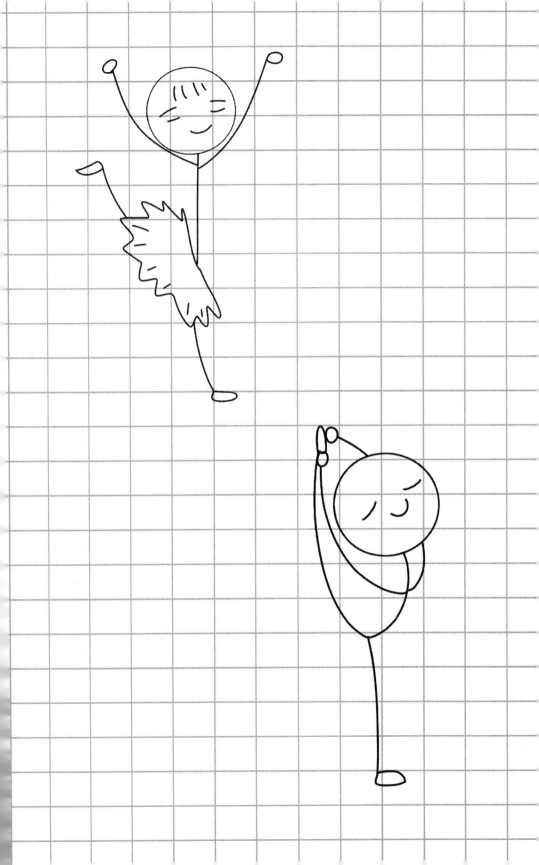

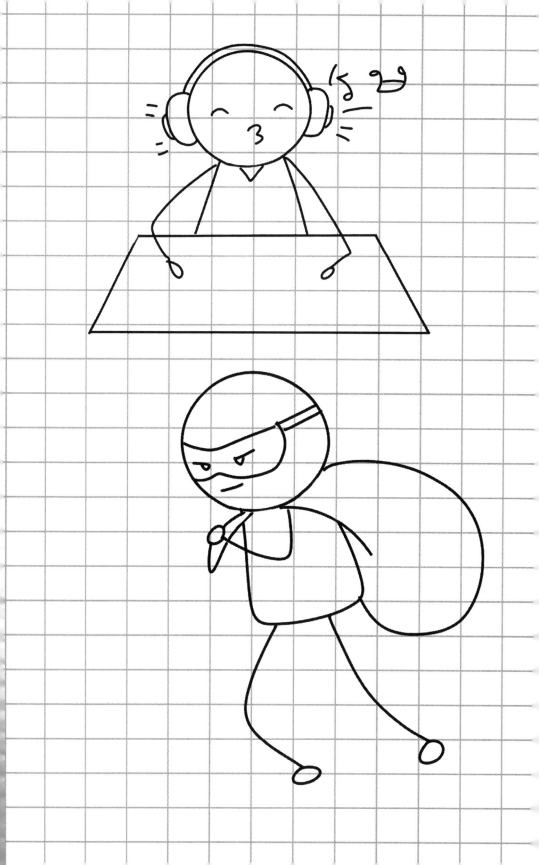

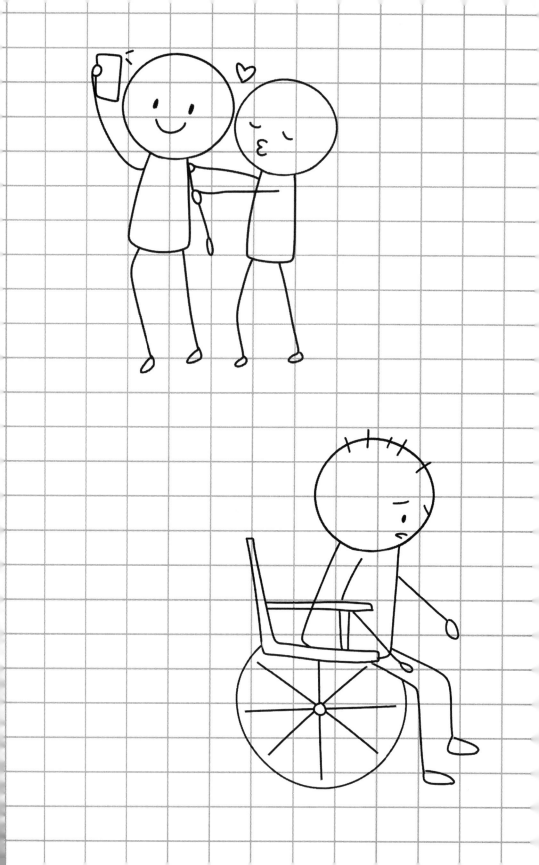

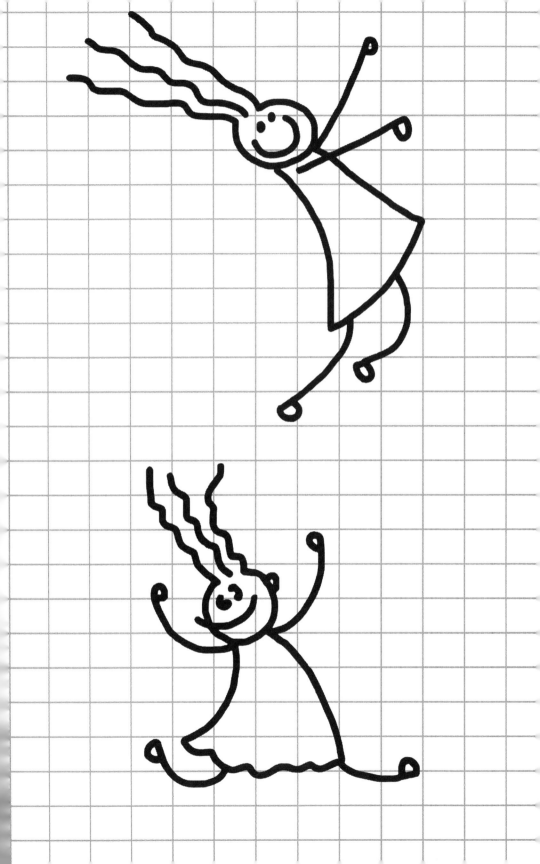

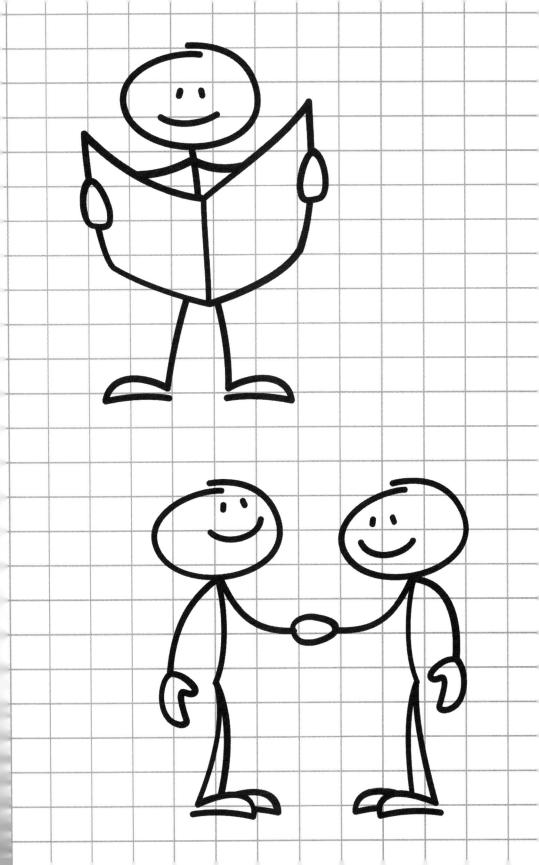

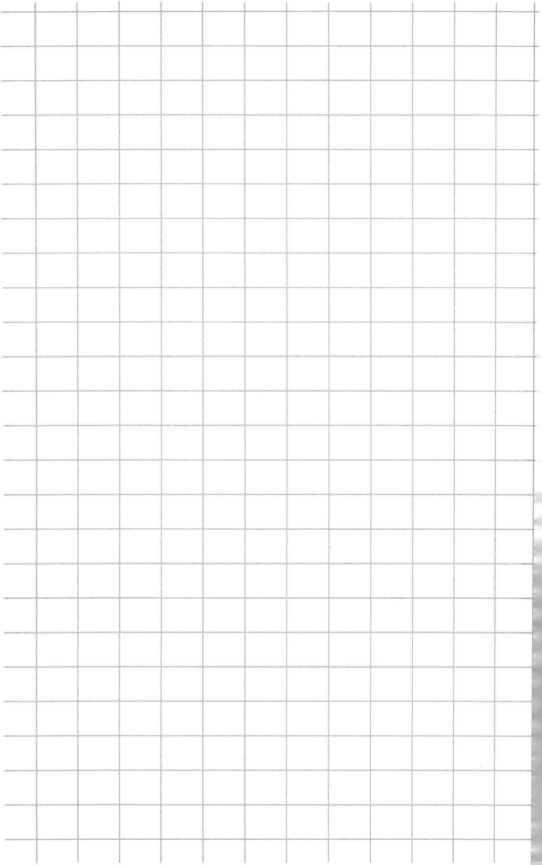

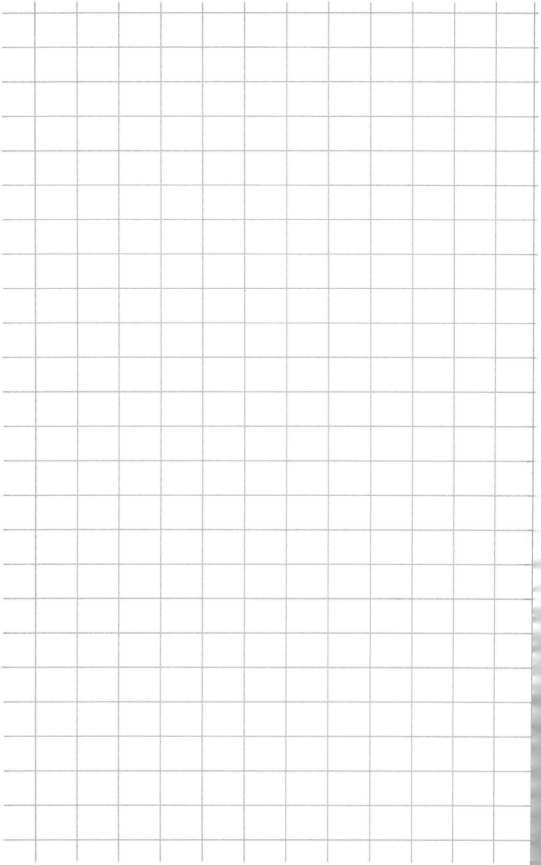

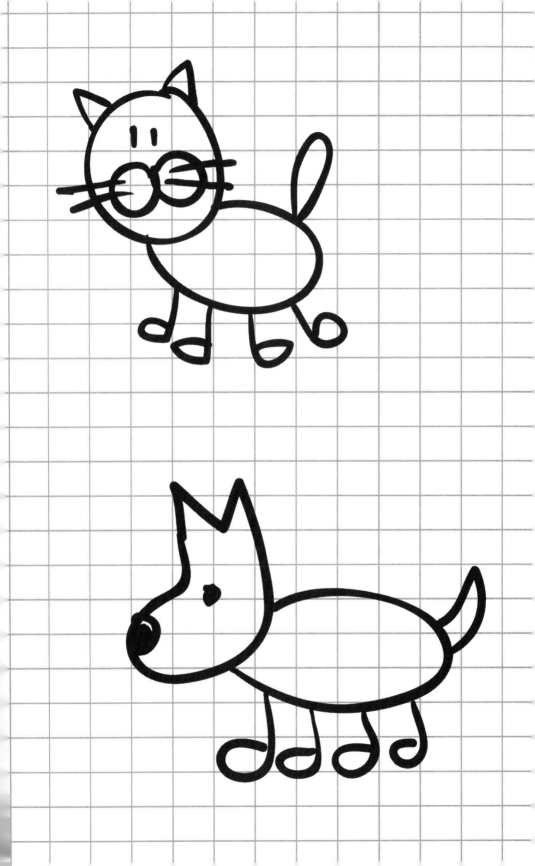

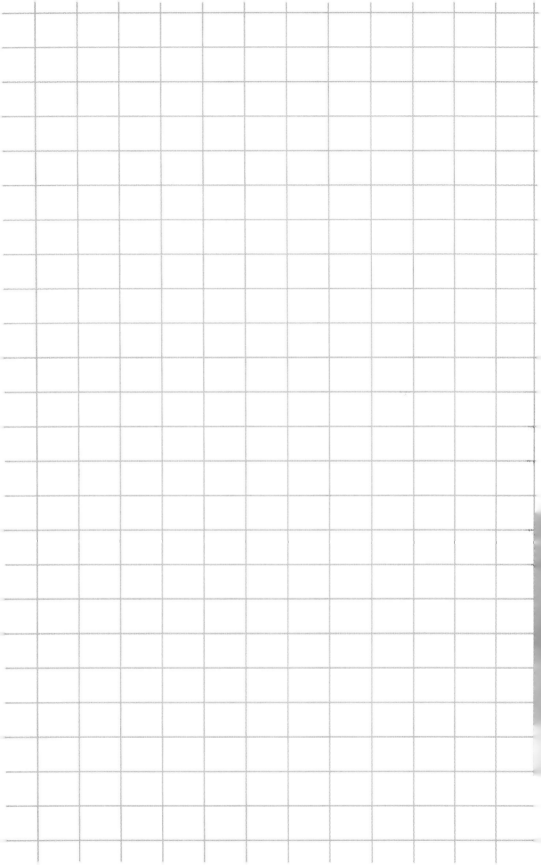

Our Publications at

Amazon.com

Our Publications at

Amazon.co.uk

Thank you for shopping at Sketch Fabrica.

If you have any questions or concerns please let us know.

We truly care about your customer experience and,

we are 100% dedicated to your complete satisfaction.

Your feedback will help us to improve our services.

We genuinely hope that your experience with our store was one that was positive and memorable.

Thank you in advance for your valuable feedback.

To leave a product review, please sign in to your Amazon account .

For any additional comments, suggestions, publication requests please do not hesitate to contact us

sketchfabrica@gmail.com

Made in the USA
Columbia, SC
16 February 2022